AF510005

Table of Contents

1 Introduction to M&A

Mergers involve the combination of two or more companies into a single entity, often resulting in a new, larger company. This process typically involves the consolidation of assets, liabilities, and operations under a unified corporate structure. Shareholders of the merging companies may receive shares in the new entity, depending on the specific terms of the merger agreement. A significant aspect to consider, which will be explored in later chapters, is the tax treatment of these transactions; different tax implications arise depending on the structure and method of the merger.

Acquisitions, on the other hand, involve one company (the acquirer) purchasing another company (the target). The acquirer may purchase all or a portion of the target's assets or stock, leading to a change in ownership. Unlike mergers, acquisitions maintain the legal existence of the acquiring entity; only the target company might cease to exist as a separate legal entity depending on the transaction structure—a key factor influencing tax implications, as we'll see.

The distinction between mergers and acquisitions, seemingly subtle, holds significant legal and financial weight. A merger represents a joining of equals, whereas an acquisition signifies one entity taking control of another. These differences significantly impact legal processes, shareholder rights, and, crucially for this book, the tax implications.

Understanding these fundamental differences is paramount. It forms the very basis upon which the subsequent chapters will build. The tax consequences arising from mergers differ dramatically from those stemming from acquisitions. Therefore, recognizing these core distinctions is the crucial first step in navigating the complex tax landscape of mergers and acquisitions. Imagine trying to build a house without laying a solid foundation—the entire structure becomes unstable. Similarly, grasping these foundational concepts allows us to build a strong understanding of the taxation involved.

Consider a scenario: Company A, with a strong brand but limited market reach, merges with Company B, possessing extensive distribution networks. The combined entity leverages Company B's infrastructure to expand Company A's market presence, realizing synergies which would be impossible otherwise. Yet, the tax consequences of this merger, including the treatment of assets and liabilities, will differ markedly from those arising if Company A had simply acquired Company B. This seemingly simple difference has profound implications in terms of tax efficiency. Proper planning from the outset is critical, as missteps can lead to significant tax liabilities.

The structural differences between mergers and acquisitions extend beyond just the legal definition. These differences determine how assets and liabilities are transferred, how shareholder interests are handled, and the subsequent tax effects. Moreover, the choice between an asset purchase or a stock purchase, for example, presents various tax consequences. A well-structured deal considers these nuances proactively, often with the assistance of experienced tax advisors.

Therefore, before embarking on the complexities of tax implications, a solid understanding of what constitutes a merger versus an acquisition is essential. We have now laid the groundwork for the more detailed exploration of tax effects within each type of transaction, which we will undertake in the following chapters. Mastering this initial differentiation is critical to understanding the detailed information that follows.

1.1 Understanding Mergers

Mergers, in their simplest form, involve the combination of two or more companies into a single entity. This isn't a simple amalgamation, however. The legal structures involved can vary widely, leading to dramatically different tax consequences. Understanding these nuances is crucial for navigating the complex legal and financial landscape. Consider, for instance, the difference between a statutory merger, where one company absorbs another, and a consolidation, where both companies cease to exist and a new entity is formed. Each carries its own unique set of tax implications, impacting everything from the tax basis of assets to the overall tax liability of the resulting firm. Ignoring these differences could lead to significant financial setbacks.

A key distinction to grasp lies in how the merger is structured. Is it a stock-for-stock exchange or a stock-for-assets transaction? In a stock-for-stock merger, shareholders of one company exchange their shares for shares in the surviving company. The tax implications here are generally minimal, as no taxable event typically occurs for the shareholders unless there's a significant difference between the market value and the basis of their shares. Conversely, in a stock-for-assets transaction, the acquiring company purchases the assets of the target company directly. This often triggers a taxable event for the target company's shareholders, requiring careful consideration of capital gains taxes and potential tax liabilities.

The process requires meticulous planning and coordination. Legal counsel specializing in mergers and acquisitions (M&A) is invaluable during this phase. They'll guide you through the necessary legal steps, ensuring compliance with all relevant regulations. Simultaneously, tax professionals will work to minimize the tax burden associated with the merger. Their expertise is not merely about calculating tax liabilities. They help strategize to structure the merger in the most tax-advantageous way. This might involve exploring opportunities for tax-free reorganizations, minimizing capital gains taxes, or optimizing depreciation and amortization deductions. The synergistic expertise of legal and tax professionals will help ensure success.

Effective communication with stakeholders is critical. Shareholders need clear and transparent communication about the merger's implications, especially concerning their tax liabilities. This avoids misunderstandings and potential legal challenges down the line. Transparency fosters trust and collaboration, which are vital for a successful merger. Remember, a well-informed shareholder is more likely to support the merger, contributing to a smoother and more efficient process, minimizing potential conflicts and resistance. It is essential to ensure everyone involved is on the same page.

Furthermore, post-merger integration involves significant tax implications. The newly merged entity must establish a consolidated tax reporting system, ensuring all tax obligations are met efficiently. This includes managing the tax bases of transferred assets, calculating depreciation and amortization deductions correctly, and navigating the intricacies of consolidated tax returns. Effective post-merger tax planning ensures that tax benefits and obligations are managed effectively, minimizing any possible problems which may surface after the merger is completed. These are crucial steps that should never be overlooked.

Beyond the immediate tax implications, consider long-term strategies. The nature of the merger can significantly shape the long-term tax profile of the merged entity. For instance, the choice of accounting methods—such as the treatment of goodwill—has significant ramifications on annual tax liabilities and overall long-term tax planning. A thorough understanding of these implications is crucial for ensuring the long-term financial health of the merged entity. This long-term approach contributes to a sustainable strategy for maximizing the benefits of the merger.

Finally, always remember that the specific tax implications of a merger will be unique to each case. Factors such as the size of the companies involved, the nature of their assets, and the structure of the merger all contribute to the overall tax landscape. There's no one-size-fits-all solution. Seeking professional tax advice tailored to your specific situation is not simply recommended; it is absolutely essential. A poorly planned merger can have profound and long-lasting negative consequences. Expert guidance ensures that you are fully prepared, making informed decisions that safeguard your financial future. Proactive tax planning is, therefore, paramount to the success of any merger.

1.2 Acquisitions Defined

An acquisition, in its simplest form, is the purchase of one company by another. This seemingly straightforward definition belies the complex web of legal, financial, and—critically—tax implications that unfold. Unlike a simple asset purchase, an acquisition often involves the acquisition of the target company's entire stock, effectively making it a subsidiary of the acquiring entity. This fundamental difference significantly shapes the tax landscape. The acquiring company doesn't just buy assets; it inherits the entire corporate structure, including liabilities, contracts, and, of course, tax history. Understanding this distinction is paramount.

This process frequently involves a significant amount of due diligence. Before a single contract is signed, legal and financial teams meticulously scrutinize every aspect of the target company. This examination goes far beyond financial statements, extending to contracts, intellectual property, environmental compliance, and potential liabilities. Tax professionals play a pivotal role, assessing the target's tax history, uncovering potential tax liabilities, and predicting future tax implications for the acquiring company. Neglecting thorough due diligence is risky, potentially leading to unexpected tax burdens and costly legal battles down the line.

The purchase price allocation is a crucial step in the post-acquisition process. It's not just a matter of assigning a lump sum to the entire business. The price must be meticulously allocated among the acquired assets, both tangible (like property, plant, and equipment) and intangible (like goodwill, trademarks, and patents). This precise allocation directly impacts future tax deductions. Assets with shorter useful lives will be depreciated more quickly, leading to higher deductions in the early years, whereas longer-lived assets will generate deductions over a longer period. The intricacies of purchase price allocation can be quite complex, often requiring specialized expertise to navigate successfully. Overlooking this crucial step can easily lead to missed tax benefits or, conversely, an overestimation of depreciation and amortization, incurring tax penalties.

Many acquisitions involve a complex interplay of stock and assets. Stock acquisitions, where the buyer purchases the target company's stock, often have different tax implications than asset acquisitions, where the buyer purchases the individual assets of the company. In a stock acquisition, the target company typically remains a separate legal entity, although now under the control of the acquiring company. This preserves the target's existing tax basis for assets, but the acquiring company might be able to file a consolidated tax return, simplifying tax reporting and potentially leading to tax efficiencies. This is in stark contrast to asset acquisitions, where the acquiring company generally takes on the tax basis of the purchased assets, and the implications of this can be quite substantial. The choice between these two paths depends greatly on the specific circumstances of the deal and a careful analysis of tax consequences.

Beyond the initial transaction itself, the long-term tax implications are substantial. Post-acquisition tax integration is an ongoing process. The acquiring company must integrate the target company's accounting systems, address any potential tax discrepancies, and ensure compliance with all relevant tax regulations. This integration involves both administrative tasks and strategic tax planning. For example, the acquiring company might need to adjust its tax planning strategy to reflect the addition of the target company's operations, potentially leading to changes in the overall tax strategy. Filing consolidated tax returns is a significant aspect of this integration; it can greatly simplify tax reporting while also creating opportunities for tax savings. Failure to manage this transition smoothly can result in costly errors and penalties.

One of the most crucial aspects of an acquisition is determining the fair market value of the acquired assets. This valuation influences the purchase price allocation and, consequently, the depreciation and amortization deductions. Accurate valuation is critical to minimizing tax liabilities and optimizing the tax benefits available to the acquiring company. Intangible assets, such as goodwill, patents, and trademarks, often pose unique challenges in valuation. Professional valuation services are often necessary to provide an objective assessment that is defendable from a tax perspective. Incorrect valuation can lead to significant tax discrepancies and potential challenges with tax authorities. An accurate valuation ensures that the tax benefits are fully realized, and ensures that the company avoids penalties due to incorrectly allocated costs.

Finally, remember that the acquisition process, like any major corporate transaction, carries potential for tax disputes. Understanding the possibilities of IRS audits and examinations is crucial. The acquiring company needs to maintain thorough documentation of the acquisition process and all related tax decisions. This documentation is critical in navigating any tax controversy. Proactive tax planning, meticulous record-keeping, and engagement with experienced tax professionals can substantially reduce the risk of disputes and mitigate the impact of any potential challenges.

Acquisitions, therefore, are not merely about acquiring assets;

they're about managing a complex web of tax considerations, from the initial due diligence to long-term tax integration. A clear understanding of the intricacies of tax implications is crucial for success.

2 Tax Implications of Mergers

Understanding the tax implications of a merger is crucial for a successful transaction. The complexities involved can be significant, demanding careful planning and expert advice from the outset. Failure to adequately address these implications can lead to unforeseen tax liabilities, jeopardizing the financial health of the merged entity. Navigating this landscape requires a clear understanding of several key areas.

A primary concern is the adjustment of tax bases. Following a merger, the assets and liabilities of the merging companies are combined. The tax basis of these assets changes, impacting future depreciation and amortization deductions. The new tax basis is typically determined by the fair market value of the assets at the time of the merger, potentially triggering capital gains or losses. Accurate valuation is therefore paramount, influencing the overall tax consequences and necessitating careful consideration of potential tax implications during negotiations. This often involves professional appraisals and meticulous record-keeping.

A critical distinction lies in choosing between an asset deal and a stock deal. In an asset deal, the acquiring company purchases the assets of the target company directly. This allows for the step-up in basis mentioned previously, potentially offering significant tax advantages. Conversely, in a stock deal, the acquiring company purchases the target company's stock. The tax basis of the assets remains unchanged, thus preserving the original tax liabilities but often avoiding the complications of individual asset valuation. The choice between these structures profoundly impacts the tax implications and requires careful weighing of the advantages and disadvantages specific to each transaction. Selecting the optimal structure should be undertaken with the guidance of legal and tax professionals, ensuring that the chosen path aligns with the overall business objectives and mitigates potential tax burdens. This strategy also impacts the future financial reporting of the newly combined entity.

Consolidated tax returns are another essential aspect of post-merger tax management. After a merger, the newly formed entity can file a consolidated return, which combines the financial information of all its subsidiaries. This simplifies the reporting process and can result in significant tax savings, reducing the overall tax burden. However, filing a consolidated return involves intricate regulations and requires careful coordination between the various entities involved. Understanding the specific requirements and regulations concerning consolidated returns is therefore paramount in minimizing tax liabilities post-merger. Such expertise usually necessitates the input of experienced tax professionals, especially when dealing with complexities such as differing accounting methods or international tax implications.

Moreover, the intricacies of state and local taxes must not be overlooked. Mergers often involve entities operating in multiple jurisdictions, creating complexities in how sales, property and other relevant taxes are handled. Careful coordination and planning are crucial to ensure compliance with all relevant state and local tax laws, preventing penalties and fines that could severely impact the merged entity's financial position. Failure to address state tax compliance adequately could result in significant liabilities and jeopardize the economic success of the combined entity. Thus, seeking expertise from tax professionals specializing in state and local tax matters is vital during the merger process. This area demands careful attention to detail, as minor oversights can lead to substantial tax liabilities.

The tax consequences of a merger are not limited to the immediate aftermath of the transaction. Long-term tax planning is critical for maintaining the financial health and profitability of the merged entity. Post-merger tax integration involves integrating different accounting systems, coordinating tax reporting, and ensuring compliance with all ongoing tax obligations. Establishing a robust post-merger tax strategy facilitates efficient tax management, minimizing future tax burdens and contributing to the overall success of the combined entity. Proactive tax planning in the long term is a crucial component of a successful merger, ensuring that the combined entity operates efficiently and sustainably. Therefore, it's prudent to include tax professionals in post-merger planning to ensure the entity maintains compliance and optimizes tax efficiency going forward. The goal isn't simply to avoid problems; it is to build a sustainable foundation for long-term profitability.

2.1 Tax Basis Adjustments

Understanding the intricacies of tax basis adjustments is crucial for successfully navigating the tax implications of mergers and acquisitions. These adjustments, often complex and nuanced, directly impact a company's tax liability post-transaction. Failure to properly account for them can lead to significant financial penalties and undermine the overall success of the deal.

The fundamental principle guiding tax basis adjustments stems from the need for consistency in reporting assets' values for tax purposes. When assets are transferred during a merger or acquisition, their tax basis—the original cost minus depreciation—often shifts. This shift is determined by the type of transaction—stock or asset deal—and the specific rules governing the transfer. Consider, for instance, a scenario where a company acquires another using its stock. In this stock acquisition, the acquiring company generally inherits the target's tax basis, maintaining continuity and avoiding immediate tax consequences. This is in stark contrast to an asset acquisition. An asset acquisition, however, presents a different landscape. Here, the acquiring company establishes a new tax basis for each acquired asset, usually aligning with the purchase price allocated to those assets. This can create both advantages and disadvantages. While it allows for the immediate depreciation of assets acquired at a higher value than their book value, it also generates a significant tax impact depending on the difference between the purchase price and the seller's book value of the assets. The ramifications are significant; proper allocation of the purchase price among the assets is crucial to optimize depreciation and amortization deductions, ultimately influencing the tax burden over the asset's lifetime.

The carryover basis, prevalent in stock acquisitions, essentially maintains the existing tax basis of the assets. The absence of an immediate tax event makes it a seemingly simpler approach. Yet, the absence of immediate tax impact needs careful consideration; it may defer tax savings which could have offset the purchase price for example, limiting financial flexibility for the acquiring firm. The implications for future tax planning are thus quite different between stock and asset acquisitions, impacting deferred tax liabilities and affecting the long-term financial strategies.

Determining the appropriate tax basis necessitates a careful review of the transaction's details. The valuation of the assets involved is paramount. Any discrepancy between the agreed-upon purchase price and the fair market value of the assets needs to be carefully allocated to ensure the tax basis is correctly adjusted. Professional valuation expertise is crucial in ensuring accuracy and minimizing the potential for disputes with the tax authorities. The allocation process itself is often complex, requiring careful consideration of intangible assets such as goodwill, intellectual property, and brand value. Each of these components requires specific and often highly technical valuation methods, each adding considerable complexity and potentially influencing the allocation results substantially.

Furthermore, the impact of tax basis adjustments extends beyond the immediate tax consequences. It can significantly affect the depreciation and amortization deductions claimed by the acquiring company in the years following the transaction. These deductions, in turn, directly impact the company's taxable income and its overall financial health. Miscalculating these adjustments can lead to inaccurate reporting, inviting potential audits and costly penalties. Therefore, meticulous attention to detail, including appropriate documentation and consulting experts are imperative. A thorough and well-documented process minimizes the risks and enhances compliance.

Therefore, meticulous planning and a deep understanding of tax laws are paramount. It necessitates expertise not just in accounting, but also a strong grasp of corporate tax law. Experienced tax professionals are invaluable resources in ensuring compliance, minimizing tax burdens, and avoiding costly errors. Their expertise extends to guiding the allocation of purchase price across the assets, thereby optimizing the future tax deductions and ensuring the long-term success of the acquisition. Investing in professional guidance is a worthwhile investment that can safeguard a deal from costly unintended tax implications.

In essence, navigating the complexities of tax basis adjustments requires a proactive, strategic approach. By comprehending the underlying principles, understanding the implications of asset versus stock acquisitions, and diligently conducting appropriate valuation and allocation, businesses can harness the power of these adjustments to optimize their tax position and ultimately increase the financial benefits of their merger or acquisition. The long-term financial health of the post-merger entity hinges on this meticulous attention to detail. Careful attention to these aspects safeguards against penalties and potentially unwanted legal implications as well. Properly managing these issues ensures that the merger or acquisition yields the desired financial and business outcomes.

2.2 Asset vs. Stock Deals

Choosing between an asset deal and a stock deal significantly impacts the tax implications of a merger or acquisition. In an asset deal, the buyer purchases the target company's individual assets, assuming liabilities separately. This allows for a detailed allocation of the purchase price across various assets, influencing depreciation and amortization deductions. This granular approach offers the opportunity for significant tax optimization, especially when dealing with assets with different depreciation schedules or tax lives. However, it's a more complex process, requiring extensive due diligence and potentially increasing transaction costs.

The stock deal, conversely, involves purchasing the target company's stock directly. This method is often faster and simpler, with less legal complexity compared to the asset deal's detailed asset-by-asset transfer. The buyer inherits all assets and liabilities, and typically takes over the seller's tax attributes. This can be advantageous if the target company has net operating losses (NOLs) that the buyer can utilize to offset future taxable income. However, this approach might limit the ability to selectively depreciate assets or claim certain tax deductions.

A key difference lies in the tax basis of assets. In an asset deal, the buyer establishes a new tax basis for each acquired asset, determined by the allocated purchase price. This is crucial for calculating depreciation and amortization deductions over the asset's useful life. In contrast, in a stock deal, the tax basis of the assets remains the same as it was on the seller's books, potentially leading to less advantageous depreciation deductions. This means potential missed opportunities for maximizing tax benefits. Careful planning and consideration of each asset's value and depreciation schedule are essential.

The legal implications also differ significantly. An asset deal involves transferring ownership of each individual asset, requiring detailed contracts and agreements for each transfer. This meticulous process involves significant legal work and review, making it time-consuming and potentially more expensive. A stock deal is less cumbersome, demanding mainly a sale and purchase agreement for the target company's shares. While quicker, the lack of detail may later create unforeseen complications.

The choice between an asset deal and a stock deal should be strategically aligned with the buyer's overall tax planning goals. If maximizing depreciation and amortization deductions is paramount, and you have the resources to navigate the complexities, an asset deal may be preferred. If a simpler, faster transaction is prioritized, perhaps utilizing the seller's existing tax attributes, a stock deal may be more suitable. It's crucial to weigh the tax benefits against the increased complexity and potential costs associated with an asset deal. The optimal choice often hinges on a detailed analysis of both the tax and legal implications, factoring in the specific circumstances of the target company and the buyer's financial objectives.

Furthermore, the presence of liabilities plays a crucial role in the decision. In an asset deal, the buyer can select which liabilities to assume, potentially excluding those that could pose a financial burden. This selective assumption of liabilities provides flexibility and allows for better risk management. In a stock deal, the buyer inherits all liabilities, which can be both a financial advantage, if the seller has valuable tax attributes, or a disadvantage, if hidden liabilities exist. Thorough due diligence is paramount to identify and assess the potential financial impacts of the liabilities.

Finally, state laws regarding sales and use taxes should also be evaluated. The purchase of assets may be subject to sales and use taxes in some jurisdictions, depending on the type of assets and the relevant state regulations. In contrast, the purchase of stock generally does not involve sales or use taxes. Failing to account for potential sales tax liabilities in an asset deal could have substantial financial repercussions. A comprehensive understanding of both federal and state tax rules is critical for making an informed decision. Ultimately, the choice requires a multi-faceted consideration, including tax implications, legal complexities, and potential financial benefits and risks. A thorough professional analysis is essential before settling on a deal structure.

2.3 Consolidated Returns

Filing consolidated returns after a merger offers significant tax advantages, but understanding the intricacies is crucial. It's not a simple switch; careful planning and adherence to specific regulations are paramount. For example, a parent company must own at least 80% of the subsidiary's stock to qualify for filing consolidated returns. This ownership threshold is determined by considering voting power and value. Ignoring this requirement can lead to severe penalties and negate the intended benefits.

The primary advantage of consolidated returns lies in the elimination of intercompany transactions. Imagine profits shifting between related entities—a common occurrence in a newly merged company. These internal transactions, taxable if treated separately, become irrelevant under a consolidated return. This simplification drastically reduces the overall tax burden by netting gains and losses. The result is a single tax liability calculated on the combined income of all entities, avoiding double taxation. Moreover, losses from one subsidiary can offset profits from another, maximizing tax savings.

However, choosing to file a consolidated return isn't without its complexities. It requires a significant amount of additional paperwork and careful coordination between accounting and legal teams. You'll need to meticulously track all intercompany transactions, ensuring accuracy across the board. Failure to maintain detailed records can lead to audits and potential penalties, undermining the very advantages the consolidated return is designed to provide. This process demands meticulous attention, as even minor discrepancies can snowball into significant compliance issues.

Furthermore, the complexities extend to the allocation of income and deductions among the entities. This requires a clear understanding of the Internal Revenue Code and its specific regulations concerning consolidated returns. Each entity's individual financial statements need to be thoroughly examined and adjusted to ensure accurate reporting. Failure to properly allocate income and expenses can distort the overall financial picture, leading to miscalculations and potentially large tax liabilities. Expert advice from a seasoned tax professional is almost always necessary.

One often-overlooked aspect is the impact on the audit process. While a consolidated return streamlines tax calculations, it also increases the scope of any potential audit. The IRS will examine the financial statements of each entity involved, making thorough record-keeping vital to defend any potential challenges. Proactive measures, such as maintaining detailed documentation for all transactions and proactively addressing potential areas of concern, can significantly minimize the risk of disputes. This proactive approach can translate to significant cost savings in the long run, by preventing costly legal battles.

Another crucial consideration is the impact on state taxes. Many states follow the federal rules for consolidated returns, but not all. It's essential to research the specific regulations in each state where the merged entities operate to ensure full compliance at all levels of governance. This involves understanding the differences in state tax laws and ensuring each entity's operations are reflected accurately on the relevant tax forms for each jurisdiction. Overlooking this can lead to significant liabilities across multiple states.

The choice to utilize consolidated returns needs careful evaluation considering the specific circumstances of the merger. The benefits of reduced tax liabilities must be carefully weighed against the increased administrative burden and the complexity of compliance procedures. This assessment requires a thorough analysis of the financial positions of all involved entities and a comprehensive understanding of all potential consequences. A proper cost-benefit analysis should be conducted before proceeding, ensuring the decision aligns with the overall long-term financial strategy. This proactive approach contributes to the success and sustained growth of the merged entity. It underscores that informed decision-making significantly reduces risks and maximizes benefits.

3 Tax Aspects of Acquisitions

Thorough due diligence is paramount before any acquisition. A comprehensive tax review, ideally conducted by experienced professionals, is essential. This involves scrutinizing the target company's tax returns for the past several years, identifying any potential tax liabilities, and assessing the company's tax compliance history. Ignoring this step can lead to unforeseen costs and complications down the line, potentially jeopardizing the entire deal. Careful examination of tax returns, including state and local filings, is vital for a complete understanding of the tax implications. This meticulous review is not simply an exercise in compliance, it is a critical risk management strategy.

Purchase price allocation (PPA) is a complex process demanding precision and expertise. It's more than just dividing the purchase price among various assets; it's a strategic exercise with significant tax implications. The allocation directly affects depreciation and amortization deductions, potentially influencing tax liabilities for years to come. For instance, assigning a higher value to intangible assets like goodwill can lead to larger amortization deductions over time, reducing the taxable income. However, an incorrect allocation can result in IRS scrutiny, leading to adjustments and penalties. Therefore, a well-defined PPA strategy, developed in consultation with tax advisors, is essential to optimize the tax outcome. Understanding the intricacies of PPA is fundamental for maximizing tax efficiency after the acquisition. This involves close collaboration with valuation specialists and tax professionals to ensure that the allocation aligns with fair market value and conforms to IRS guidelines. Careful consideration of various asset categories is crucial, and documentation must be comprehensive and robust enough to withstand potential audits.

Understanding the tax basis of acquired assets is fundamental. The tax basis, essentially the value assigned to an asset for tax purposes, influences depreciation, amortization, and ultimately, tax liabilities. Different acquisition structures result in different tax bases. For example, in a stock acquisition, the buyer generally inherits the target company's existing tax basis. In contrast, an asset acquisition allows for a step-up or step-down in the tax basis to the purchase price, creating opportunities for tax optimization or leading to increased tax liabilities depending on the specifics of the transaction. Accurate determination of the tax basis is vital for post-acquisition tax planning and maximizing deductions. Proper documentation and record-keeping are crucial in supporting the calculated tax basis in the event of an audit.

Careful consideration of the legal structure of the acquisition is essential. The choice of structure—whether a stock purchase or an asset purchase—significantly influences the tax consequences. A stock acquisition generally maintains the existing corporate structure, streamlining the process but potentially limiting tax benefits. In contrast, an asset acquisition can provide greater flexibility in terms of tax benefits but can also be more complex and time-consuming. Other options, like a Section 338(h)(10) election, are available for smaller acquisitions, and its implications need to be thoroughly understood. This careful analysis of available structures, taking into account the various tax implications, allows the involved parties to develop a tax strategy that minimizes tax liability and optimizes the overall financial results. Each structure presents its unique set of advantages and disadvantages, and choosing the appropriate structure requires considerable knowledge and expertise. Thus, selecting the right structure is a critical decision that impacts the long-term tax profile of the acquiring company.

Post-acquisition tax compliance is just as crucial as pre-acquisition planning. Integrating the tax systems of two companies requires careful consideration. Consolidated tax returns, where applicable, should be filed accurately and promptly. Compliance not only minimizes penalties and interest but also ensures the long-term financial health of the combined entity. Accurate record-keeping and proper documentation are not just formalities—they are safeguards against potential audit issues and disputes with the tax authorities. Ignoring post-acquisition tax compliance can have severe financial repercussions. This includes maintaining detailed records of all transactions, ensuring consistent adherence to tax regulations, and establishing a robust system for tax reporting. Regular review of tax filings and adherence to post-merger tax planning are integral to long-term success.

3.1 Due Diligence & Tax Review

Thorough due diligence is paramount before any acquisition. Imagine buying a house without an inspection; the risks are immense. Similarly, acquiring a company without a comprehensive tax review could lead to unforeseen liabilities and lost opportunities. This isn't merely about avoiding penalties; it's about maximizing value and ensuring a smooth post-acquisition integration. A meticulous tax review identifies potential tax exposures, allowing for proactive mitigation strategies before the deal closes.

The initial phase involves examining the target company's historical tax returns, scrutinizing every detail. We're looking for discrepancies, inconsistencies, and potential areas of concern. This might include unrecorded liabilities, questionable deductions, or even possible tax evasion. Identifying these issues early allows for negotiation adjustments to the purchase price, protecting the buyer's investment. Don't underestimate the power of a detailed financial history; it's your compass in the labyrinth of corporate accounting.

A key aspect of due diligence centers around understanding the target's tax positions. Are there pending audits or ongoing disputes with the IRS? Unresolved tax matters can significantly impact the valuation and overall attractiveness of the target company. These pending liabilities, even those seemingly insignificant, can snowball into substantial financial burdens after the acquisition. Therefore, proactive identification and assessment are crucial.

Beyond the historical tax returns, reviewing current tax compliance is equally important. Are all necessary tax filings up-to-date? Are the proper tax elections in place? This assessment prevents future complications, saving time, money, and potential legal entanglements. Often overlooked, this process is where many silent problems lie, ready to surface with devastating consequences post-acquisition. It's preventative maintenance of the highest order for any business combination.

Purchase price allocation, a crucial step, requires determining the fair market value of each acquired asset. This process directly impacts depreciation and amortization deductions, which influence the tax liability in future periods. Accurate allocation is a complex process requiring expertise in valuation and tax law, ensuring the most favorable tax position. It involves not just tangible assets like equipment, but also intangible assets like goodwill, intellectual property, and customer lists. Each component needs precise valuation.

Furthermore, understanding the target company's tax structure is essential. Is it a corporation, partnership, or LLC? This seemingly simple question affects how taxes are paid and filed. The differences in how each entity handles taxation can dramatically affect the overall tax burden. Ignoring these structural differences can lead to costly mistakes and compliance issues. The implications are significant for the acquiring company's overall tax strategy post-merger.

Don't underestimate the role of experienced tax professionals. Their expertise in navigating the intricacies of tax law is invaluable during due diligence and beyond. They can identify potential issues, provide strategic advice, and help structure the deal to minimize tax liabilities, avoiding potentially disastrous financial consequences. They bring a depth of knowledge that safeguards against unknown risks, a safety net for a sometimes unpredictable field. Their assistance provides clarity in complex financial issues.

Finally, the tax review should extend beyond the current tax year. Projections of future tax liabilities should be incorporated, offering a clearer picture of the long-term tax implications of the acquisition. This foresight is crucial for strategic financial planning and ensures that the buyer isn't blindsided by unexpected tax expenses in the years following the acquisition. It allows informed decision-making and positions the newly formed entity for ongoing success. The long-term picture is just as crucial as the initial analysis.

3.2 Purchase Price Allocation

Accurate purchase price allocation (PPA) is paramount in mergers and acquisitions (M&A). It's not merely a post-acquisition accounting exercise; it significantly influences tax liabilities for years to come, impacting depreciation and amortization deductions. Getting it wrong can lead to substantial penalties and adjustments from the IRS, highlighting the crucial need for meticulous planning and expert guidance. This often overlooked detail can make or break a deal's long-term financial health.

Consider a scenario where a company acquires another for $100 million. Simply recording this as the total cost isn't sufficient. The acquiring company must allocate that $100 million across the acquired assets, including tangible assets like equipment and property, and intangible assets like customer lists, brand names, and intellectual property. This allocation directly impacts the depreciation schedules and amortization periods assigned to each asset. A misallocation can result in significantly understating or overstating depreciation expenses, directly affecting the company's taxable income.

The process demands a thorough understanding of fair market value. Determining this value for tangible assets is typically straightforward using appraisal methods and market comparisons. However, valuing intangible assets requires a more sophisticated approach. Methods like discounted cash flow (DCF) analysis, relief from royalty (RRR) and market approaches are often used to arrive at a reasonable estimate. These methods are complex and require specialized expertise in valuation, which is why securing the services of a qualified valuation professional is essential. It is a multistep process, carefully weighing the factors impacting value and using multiple valuation approaches.

Intangible asset valuation requires even greater care and precision. This is because many acquired intangible assets do not have easily accessible market comparables. The valuation of customer relationships, brand names, and intellectual property often involves detailed analyses of their expected future economic benefits. This can prove challenging, especially in cases involving a complex interplay of multiple intangible assets contributing to the overall value of the acquired company. The choice of an appropriate valuation method will depend on the specific characteristics of each intangible asset.

Beyond valuation, the PPA process involves meticulous documentation. The allocation must be justified by supporting evidence such as appraisals, market data, and internal financial records. This comprehensive documentation is crucial not only for tax purposes but also for defending the allocation in case of an IRS audit. The documentation should demonstrate that the allocation was performed using sound accounting principles and reflects the fair market values of the acquired assets. A well-prepared PPA report, comprehensive in its detail and justification, acts as a strong defense.

Furthermore, the allocation impacts the tax basis of each asset, which subsequently impacts the depreciation and amortization deductions. Accelerated depreciation might be possible on certain assets, enabling greater tax savings in the early years. The implications of this are significant, because minimizing your tax liability in the early years can lead to enhanced cash flow, which can be reinvested into the business. This will allow for more rapid growth and development of the business, which should be the goal of any M&A transaction.

Remember, PPA isn't a one-time event; its impact extends throughout the useful life of the acquired assets. Inaccurate allocation can lead to prolonged tax issues, requiring complex adjustments and potentially significant penalties. This is why professional assistance from tax and accounting experts specializing in M&A is essential. Their expertise ensures compliance with tax regulations and minimizes the risk of future audits and penalties.

Therefore, proper PPA is not simply a compliance requirement, it's a strategic element in maximizing the tax benefits of an acquisition. The process involves a detailed analysis, valuation of tangible and intangible assets, and comprehensive documentation. By understanding the intricacies of PPA, businesses can leverage it for tax optimization and ensure long-term financial health after completing an M&A transaction. The consequences of neglecting this critical step can far outweigh the initial cost of employing qualified professionals, demonstrating that preparation is key to a successful post-merger integration.

Careful planning, thorough valuation, and comprehensive documentation are crucial to protecting your interests and ensuring a smooth tax compliance post-acquisition.

4 Structuring for Tax Efficiency

Careful structuring is paramount for minimizing tax liabilities in mergers and acquisitions. Understanding the intricacies of various transaction structures is key, impacting not only immediate tax burdens but also long-term tax efficiency. A poorly structured deal can lead to unforeseen tax penalties and diminished shareholder value. Therefore, seeking expert advice is crucial during the planning stages.

Section 338(h)(10) elections provide a powerful tool for achieving tax efficiency in certain acquisitions. By electing this provision, a buyer can treat the acquisition as an asset purchase for tax purposes, even if structured as a stock purchase legally. This allows for stepped-up basis on the acquired assets, leading to increased depreciation and amortization deductions, effectively reducing future tax liabilities. However, it's crucial to carefully evaluate the circumstances; this election isn't always beneficial, demanding a thorough cost-benefit analysis. The complexities inherent necessitate professional tax advice.

Tax-free reorganizations offer significant tax advantages. These transactions, conforming to specific Internal Revenue Code requirements, allow for the transfer of assets or stock without triggering immediate tax consequences. This strategy preserves capital and defers tax payments until a later date, potentially significantly benefiting the shareholders involved. However, adhering to the strict rules governing tax-free reorganizations is essential; any deviation can result in unfavorable tax outcomes. Leveraged buyouts (LBOs), often involving substantial debt financing, require careful tax planning. Interest deductions on the borrowed funds can be substantial, reducing taxable income. However, intricate rules govern the deductibility of interest expenses; failing to comply meticulously with these regulations can negate the tax benefits. Strategic planning for debt allocation and repayment schedules is critical for successful LBO tax optimization. It requires a nuanced understanding of financial and tax laws.

Spin-offs and divestitures present opportunities for tax-efficient restructuring. A spin-off involves separating a subsidiary into a new, independent entity, potentially resulting in tax benefits for both the parent and the newly formed company. Similarly, divestitures allow for the disposal of unprofitable or non-core business assets, enabling a strategic tax planning move that minimizes tax burdens. Yet, these transactions often require meticulous planning to avoid triggering unintended tax liabilities. It's essential to consult experienced professionals who can guide you in the complexities of tax legislation related to spin-offs and divestitures.

International tax considerations introduce a whole new layer of complexity for cross-border transactions. Tax treaties, differing tax rates, and transfer pricing regulations can significantly impact tax liabilities. Careful planning, including structuring the deal strategically to minimize international tax exposure, is essential. Navigating these complex international tax regulations demands expertise in both international tax law and the specific tax laws of the countries involved. Improper planning in cross-border transactions can lead to substantial tax liabilities and financial difficulties. It's advised to utilize the services of a specialized international tax advisor to navigate these issues efficiently.

The choice of the most efficient structure depends heavily on the specific circumstances of each merger or acquisition. Factors such as the relative values of the businesses involved, their financial health, the desired level of control, and the overall business objectives of the merging entities all influence the optimal tax strategy. A comprehensive understanding of the nuances of each type of transaction is critical before selecting a specific approach. In short, selecting the best strategy necessitates a holistic approach.
Ultimately, effective tax planning in M&A transactions requires a multi-disciplinary approach. Collaboration between tax professionals, legal counsel, and financial advisors is vital to developing and implementing a robust and efficient tax strategy. Ignoring the potential tax ramifications of different structuring options can lead to significant financial disadvantages. Therefore, proactive and comprehensive tax planning from the outset is absolutely indispensable for success in the complex world of mergers and acquisitions. It's not just a matter of compliance, but of maximizing profitability and securing long-term financial stability.

4.1 Section 338(h)(10) Elections

Section 338(h)(10) elections offer a powerful tool for structuring acquisitions, allowing a buyer to achieve the tax benefits of an asset purchase while maintaining the legal structure of a stock purchase. This is particularly advantageous when dealing with smaller corporations, as it simplifies the process and minimizes potential complications. Understanding its intricacies is key to maximizing tax efficiency.
The core benefit lies in the ability to step up the basis of the target company's assets. In a traditional stock purchase, the buyer inherits the target's existing tax basis, potentially resulting in lower depreciation deductions. A 338(h)(10) election, however,

allows the buyer to treat the transaction as an asset purchase for tax purposes, thus enabling a higher basis and increased depreciation deductions, leading to significant tax savings over the life of the assets. This is particularly valuable when the target company holds assets with a low tax basis but a high fair market value. The increased depreciation translates into lower taxable income, directly impacting the bottom line.

However, this strategy isn't without its prerequisites. A key requirement is the involvement of an affiliated group of corporations. The buyer must be part of such a group, and the target corporation must be acquired entirely. This structure ensures the seamless transfer of tax benefits within the consolidated return. The election must be made within a specific timeframe, typically shortly after the acquisition closes, and requires careful planning and coordination between legal and tax advisors. Failure to meet these stringent conditions can negate the intended benefits and lead to unintended tax consequences.

Moreover, the election may lead to increased tax liabilities in the short term. The immediate step-up in basis generates a larger taxable gain for the seller. Careful negotiation and structuring, including the use of installment sales, can help mitigate this potential burden. This requires understanding the seller's specific tax circumstances and goals and coordinating the transaction details to achieve mutually beneficial results. It highlights the importance of experienced tax professionals handling these complex transactions.

Furthermore, there are nuances related to liabilities. Like any asset purchase, the buyer assumes the target's liabilities. However, the ability to deduct these liabilities varies depending on the specifics of the transaction. A thorough due diligence process is vital in assessing the potential liabilities and properly planning their tax implications. This process includes scrutinizing financial statements, reviewing contractual obligations and evaluating any potential environmental liabilities.

The process requires meticulous documentation and compliance. The IRS scrutinizes these elections, so clear and comprehensive documentation of the transaction, including the election itself, is crucial for defending against potential audits. This documentation should include supporting evidence to ensure that all aspects of the acquisition and the election are properly justified. Working closely with legal and tax professionals from the outset is crucial for successful navigation.

Ultimately, a successful 338(h)(10) election requires a coordinated strategy that balances the immediate tax implications with long-term benefits. The short-term costs might initially seem daunting, but the increased depreciation over the asset's lifetime often makes it a highly effective tax-planning tool. A thorough understanding of the election's mechanics, coupled with professional guidance, is essential for a well-informed decision. Ignoring even minor details can have significant tax repercussions. It's a powerful tool, but it demands careful execution.

4.2 Tax-Free Reorganizations

Understanding tax-free reorganizations is crucial for minimizing tax liabilities during mergers and acquisitions. These transactions, governed by Section 368 of the Internal Revenue Code, allow businesses to combine without triggering immediate tax consequences on the exchanged assets. The key is to meet specific requirements, ensuring the transaction qualifies under one of the several reorganization types. Failure to comply with these intricate rules can lead to significant unforeseen tax burdens, undermining the financial benefits of the merger or acquisition. Unlike taxable acquisitions where assets are sold and the acquiring company recognizes a gain or loss, reorganizations maintain continuity of business enterprise. This continuity is the cornerstone of tax-free treatment, meaning the transfer of assets doesn't generate a taxable event for either the acquiring or target company. The focus shifts from asset-level taxation to the overall structure and ongoing business operations. It's a nuanced area that often necessitates expert legal and accounting advice.

Several types of reorganizations exist, each with unique criteria. Type A reorganizations involve a statutory merger or consolidation, essentially combining two or more companies into a single entity. Type B reorganizations involve the acquisition of stock in exchange for voting stock of the acquiring company. A crucial element here is that the acquiring company must obtain at least 80% control of the target company. Type C reorganizations are similar to Type B, but instead of acquiring stock, the acquiring company purchases substantially all the assets of the target company in exchange for its stock. These distinctions are vital and impact the tax ramifications significantly.

Type D reorganizations involve a divisive merger, where a single company splits into two or more separate entities. This is distinctly different from the others, focusing on a split-off or split-up scenario, each with its own tax implications and requirements for maintaining nonrecognition of gain or loss. Lastly, Type E and F reorganizations involve relatively simpler changes within a corporate structure, such as recapitalizations and mergers of subsidiaries. Understanding the subtle differences between these types is essential for proper planning and execution.

Careful planning is paramount before initiating any reorganization. Tax professionals should be involved from the outset, analyzing the specific circumstances and guiding the transaction to meet the stringent requirements for tax-free status. This proactive approach ensures compliance and minimizes the risk of triggering unexpected tax liabilities. Ignoring this crucial step can lead to substantial tax penalties and negate the intended financial advantages.

The valuation of assets involved is a key consideration. While the transfer itself may be tax-free, inaccuracies in asset valuation can have downstream consequences. For example, an incorrect valuation of assets can impact depreciation and amortization deductions in the future, leading to discrepancies in tax reporting and potential audits. Therefore, a meticulous and accurate valuation process, ideally conducted by independent appraisers, is vital.

Post-reorganization, continued compliance is essential. Maintaining meticulous records and accurate reporting is crucial, preventing future audits and potential disputes with the tax authorities. This includes carefully documenting the entire process, from initial planning to the final integration of the entities. Proactive compliance minimizes the risk of future penalties and ensures the long-term success of the reorganization. Often overlooked is the ongoing monitoring of the business's financial position to identify any potential areas of non-compliance.

Successfully navigating a tax-free reorganization requires a deep understanding of intricate tax laws, meticulous planning, and close collaboration with tax professionals. The potential benefits—avoiding significant tax liabilities—are substantial. However, the complexities involved demand expertise to ensure compliance and the realization of the intended tax advantages. Understanding these intricacies is crucial, not only for minimizing immediate tax obligations but also for ensuring the continued tax efficiency of the merged or reorganized entity. The long-term implications of a well-executed tax-free reorganization far outweigh the initial effort required for careful planning and execution. Remember, seeking professional advice is not merely a suggestion but a necessity when undertaking such complex transactions. The potential pitfalls are considerable, and expert guidance can help avoid costly mistakes.

4.3 Leveraged Buyouts (LBOs)

Leveraged buyouts, or LBOs, represent a unique acquisition strategy heavily reliant on debt financing. Imagine a scenario: a private equity firm identifies a stable, profitable company with strong cash flow but potentially undervalued in the market. They structure a deal where a significant portion of the purchase price is funded by borrowed money, often secured against the acquired company's assets. The remaining portion comes from equity contributions from the private equity firm itself. This high-leverage approach amplifies returns for the equity investors but also carries substantial financial risk, making due diligence and strategic tax planning even more critical.

The tax implications of an LBO are complex and multifaceted, demanding careful consideration at every stage. Unlike straightforward asset or stock acquisitions, the debt financing significantly alters the tax landscape. Interest expense, for instance, can be deducted against the acquired company's income, potentially reducing taxable profits in the short term. However, this deduction isn't unlimited; limitations on interest deductions under Section 163(j) of the Internal Revenue Code could significantly impact the ultimate tax liability. This necessitates a thorough analysis of the company's financial structure and projected cash flow to determine the optimal debt-to-equity ratio, balancing tax benefits against the risk of financial distress.

A crucial aspect of LBO tax planning involves optimizing the purchase price allocation. Accurately allocating the purchase price among tangible and intangible assets is vital. This allocation directly affects depreciation and amortization deductions, influencing the taxable income in subsequent years. Misallocations can lead to significant tax liabilities down the line, illustrating the importance of employing experienced tax professionals in conducting this process meticulously. The accuracy of this allocation hinges upon thorough due diligence, including a comprehensive review of the target company's financial statements, intellectual property portfolio, and other assets.

Moreover, the tax treatment of any goodwill or other intangible assets acquired in an LBO deserves particular attention. Goodwill, often a significant component of the purchase price in LBO transactions, is not amortizable under current tax law. However, if any of the intangible assets have a finite life, proper determination of their useful life can lead to larger amortization deductions, lowering taxable income and improving overall tax efficiency. The careful and precise identification and valuation of these assets are imperative, requiring detailed expertise from experienced appraisers, tax professionals and accounting firms.

Structuring the LBO transaction itself also has significant tax ramifications. The choice between a stock purchase and an asset purchase drastically impacts the tax consequences for both the buyer and the seller. A stock purchase generally results in a capital gains tax liability for the seller, while an asset purchase can lead to a mix of capital gains and ordinary income, depending on the nature of the assets being sold. The tax ramifications of each approach must be weighed carefully against the overall business objectives and risk tolerance of the investors.

Post-acquisition tax planning is equally crucial in an LBO context. The acquired company might need to adjust its accounting methods to comply with the buyer's existing systems. Consolidated tax returns could provide tax benefits, but require careful integration of diverse financial reporting structures and practices. Furthermore, ongoing compliance with tax regulations is paramount, necessitating meticulous record-keeping, timely filings, and proactive tax management. Failure to adhere to these post-acquisition requirements can result in significant penalties and tax disputes with the authorities. This underscores the need for long-term tax planning, extending beyond the initial acquisition stage.

Finally, the involvement of skilled legal and tax advisors is absolutely non-negotiable in an LBO transaction. These professionals bring specialized knowledge of the complex tax regulations and financial instruments involved in these high-stakes deals. Their guidance ensures compliance with all applicable laws and regulations, mitigating the risk of significant penalties and tax disputes. Choosing advisors with proven experience in LBO transactions is essential, as their expertise can prove invaluable in navigating the intricate tax implications of such a complex financial undertaking. The success of an LBO depends not only on the financial soundness of the acquisition but also on a deep understanding and thorough management of the accompanying tax consequences.

4.4 Spin-offs and Divestiture

Spin-offs and divestitures offer distinct tax advantages, particularly when strategically planned. A spin-off involves separating a subsidiary into a new, independent company, distributing shares of the new entity to the parent company's shareholders. This can unlock value by allowing the market to separately assess the worth of each business, often leading to higher valuations than if they remained combined. Tax implications vary significantly depending on the structure chosen and the specific circumstances, and proper planning is crucial to minimize tax liabilities. It's vital to consult with tax professionals early in the process.

Careful consideration must be given to the allocation of assets and liabilities between the parent and the newly formed entity. This allocation directly impacts the tax basis of the assets in both companies, influencing future depreciation and amortization deductions. Inaccurate allocation can lead to significant tax disadvantages down the line, potentially resulting in increased tax burdens and penalties. Therefore, precise valuation and meticulous record-keeping are paramount. Consultants specializing in valuation and tax can aid in this complex process.

Divestiture, on the other hand, entails the sale or liquidation of a subsidiary or business unit. Unlike a spin-off, the parent company receives direct proceeds from the sale. This brings immediate liquidity but also incurs capital gains taxes on the sale proceeds, unless a tax-free reorganization is structured. The choice between a spin-off and a divestiture depends on various factors, including the parent company's financial goals, the market's perception of the separated entity, and the desired level of control.

Several factors influence the choice between these two options. For instance, if the parent company seeks to retain some level of control and ongoing participation in the separated business, a spin-off might be preferred. However, if the goal is simply to raise cash and disengage from a non-core business segment, a divestiture would likely be more suitable. A thorough analysis of the potential tax implications, financial ramifications, and strategic objectives is needed before deciding. This involves meticulous financial modeling, market analysis, and a deep understanding of tax regulations.

Tax planning for spin-offs and divestitures is a complex endeavor, requiring a multi-disciplinary approach. Tax professionals must work in tandem with financial advisors, legal counsel, and business strategists to develop a plan that aligns with overall business objectives and minimizes tax liabilities. This integrated approach ensures that the transaction is structured in the most tax-efficient manner while aligning with regulatory requirements and corporate governance principles. Thorough due diligence is crucial, and failure to consider all aspects can lead to costly mistakes.

A critical aspect of tax planning is determining the appropriate method of accounting for the transaction. The choice of accounting method can drastically impact the tax basis of assets, the recognition of gains or losses, and the timing of tax payments. Careful consideration must be given to the impact of different accounting standards and regulations, as well as potential differences in accounting practices across jurisdictions. It is important to understand the intricacies of tax regulations concerning both domestic and international transactions.

Furthermore, the documentation supporting the transaction

must be meticulous and comprehensive. Detailed records, including valuations, asset allocation schedules, and legal agreements, are essential not only for complying with tax regulations but also for defending against potential tax audits. The level of detail in the documentation directly impacts the likelihood of a smooth tax audit and the potential defense against any challenges raised by the tax authorities. Clear, concise, and well-organized documentation is invaluable.

Planning for potential tax audits is an essential component of successful spin-off and divestiture strategies. Understanding the potential areas of scrutiny and preparing the necessary documentation in advance can significantly reduce the risk and cost associated with audits. Moreover, proactive engagement with the tax authorities can be beneficial, fostering transparency and minimizing the likelihood of disputes. Engaging experienced tax professionals significantly improves your preparedness and reduces potential liabilities.

International tax considerations become especially significant when the spun-off entity or divested business has operations or assets in multiple jurisdictions. Understanding the tax laws and regulations of all relevant countries is crucial, including tax treaties, transfer pricing rules, and foreign tax credits. Compliance failures in this area can have severe consequences, ranging from significant tax liabilities to legal penalties. The complexities involved necessitate consulting with experts proficient in international taxation.

In summary, spin-offs and divestitures present opportunities for significant tax advantages, but successful execution requires meticulous planning, a comprehensive understanding of relevant tax laws, and a coordinated approach involving various professional advisors. Failure to address these aspects adequately can lead to unforeseen tax burdens, potential audits, and lost financial opportunities. Proactive and thorough planning is the key to successfully navigating the complexities of these business transactions. The expertise of experienced tax professionals is invaluable during the entire process, ensuring optimal tax outcomes and minimizing risks.

4.5 International Tax Considerations

Cross-border mergers and acquisitions introduce a whole new layer of complexity, significantly impacting the tax implications. Navigating these international tax considerations requires careful planning and a deep understanding of relevant treaties and regulations. Failure to do so can lead to substantial financial penalties and protracted legal battles.

Understanding the tax laws of both the acquiring and target company's jurisdictions is paramount. These laws can differ significantly, encompassing everything from corporate tax rates to withholding taxes on dividends and interest. Tax treaties, designed to prevent double taxation, play a critical role. However, the specifics of these treaties vary greatly, and interpretation can be subjective, often necessitating expert guidance.

For example, consider a US company acquiring a UK-based firm. The US tax code will treat the acquisition differently than the UK tax code. The treatment of capital gains, depreciation deductions, and the allocation of purchase price to various assets will differ under each jurisdiction's rules. The presence of a tax treaty between the US and UK might mitigate double taxation but doesn't eliminate the need for careful planning and compliance with both countries' regulations.

One crucial aspect is determining the residency status of the entities involved. The residency rules of each country determine the applicable tax rates and filing requirements. Often, a company's residency is not straightforward, particularly when dealing with multinational corporations with complex ownership structures. Careful due diligence is critical to accurately determine the applicable tax residency. A misjudgment in this area can have significant consequences.

Furthermore, the structure of the acquisition itself significantly influences the tax outcome. A stock purchase, for example, often differs considerably from an asset purchase, leading to varying tax implications in both the acquiring and acquired jurisdictions. In some instances, careful structuring of the deal can reduce overall tax burden by leveraging specific provisions within bilateral tax treaties.

Transfer pricing, a critical consideration in any multinational transaction, becomes particularly complex in M&A deals. Transfer pricing refers to the pricing of goods and services exchanged between related entities. This pricing must align with arm's-length principles—that is, it should be consistent with what unrelated parties would agree upon. If not properly documented and justified, the tax authorities of either jurisdiction can adjust the transfer prices, leading to increased tax liabilities. This necessitates robust documentation and a thorough understanding of the OECD's transfer pricing guidelines.

Beyond corporate tax rates and treaty benefits, various other taxes come into play. These may include withholding taxes on dividends, interest, and royalties; stamp duties on transaction documents; and possibly even value-added tax (VAT) on certain aspects of the acquisition process. Each jurisdiction will have its own set of rules, further adding to the complexity.

Planning for these international tax implications doesn't just involve understanding the technicalities; it requires proactive strategy. This often involves structuring the deal to minimize overall tax liabilities, maximizing the utilization of tax treaties, and establishing robust transfer pricing policies, supported by comprehensive documentation that withstands potential scrutiny from tax authorities. This should begin long before the deal closes, as it's an iterative process requiring collaboration between tax advisors, legal counsel, and deal negotiators.

Finally, remember, compliance is not merely about minimizing immediate tax liability; it's about establishing long-term tax efficiency and avoiding future disputes. Maintaining detailed and organized records of all transactions and ensuring meticulous compliance with the reporting requirements of all relevant jurisdictions is crucial. This might require establishing a robust tax compliance system that can effectively integrate the post-merger entities, aligning their tax accounting and reporting methodologies. Proactive engagement with tax authorities in both jurisdictions can also help prevent misunderstandings and potential disputes. Ignoring these aspects could lead to severe consequences, including significant fines, penalties, and protracted legal challenges. A proactive and well-informed approach is crucial for navigating the intricacies of international tax in mergers and acquisitions.

5 Post-Merger Tax Integration

Efficient post-merger tax integration is crucial for maximizing the financial benefits of an acquisition. Ignoring this aspect can lead to costly errors and missed opportunities, significantly impacting the long-term success of the combined entity. Careful planning and execution are paramount.

Immediate attention should be paid to consolidating the tax departments of both organizations. This integration goes beyond simply combining personnel; it necessitates a complete review and harmonization of accounting systems, tax reporting procedures, and internal controls. Inconsistencies in these areas can cause significant compliance headaches down the line, delaying tax filings and increasing the risk of audits. A phased approach, starting with identifying key differences and prioritizing their resolution, can be effective.

Understanding the implications of the chosen acquisition structure—whether asset or stock—is crucial. A thorough understanding of the tax basis of the acquired assets or the stock itself directly influences depreciation, amortization, and other deductions available to the combined entity. Miscalculations in this area can result in substantial tax liabilities that could have been avoided with proper planning. It's beneficial to have a tax professional experienced in M&A review these documents.

Beyond the immediate technicalities, effective communication is paramount throughout the entire process. Open and transparent communication between the tax teams, financial leadership, and legal counsel ensures that everyone understands their roles and responsibilities. This collaborative approach reduces misunderstandings and facilitates a smoother transition, minimizing disruptions to day-to-day operations. This can involve regular meetings and transparent communication channels.

One often-overlooked element is the review and potential restructuring of intercompany transactions. If the acquired company had existing transactions with affiliated entities, those will need to be re-evaluated under the new corporate structure. This review can identify opportunities for tax optimization or, conversely, reveal potential tax risks that need to be mitigated. Failing to address these intercompany relationships can lead to significant tax liabilities later on.

Post-merger tax compliance goes beyond the filing of consolidated tax returns. It requires a commitment to ongoing monitoring and meticulous record-keeping. This includes maintaining accurate documentation of all transactions, ensuring proper segregation of duties, and establishing robust internal control mechanisms to prevent errors and fraud. Regular internal audits are crucial for detecting and correcting any inconsistencies before they become significant issues. External audits will be less surprising.

The post-merger period represents a critical juncture for the combined entity. Decisions made during this time regarding tax integration will have lasting consequences, impacting the overall financial performance and long-term viability. Proactive tax planning, coupled with meticulous compliance and reporting, is not merely a cost of doing business but a strategic investment in the future success of the merged company. Thorough due diligence and experienced professional guidance are your best allies in successfully navigating this complex landscape. Ignoring these steps risks significant financial penalties.

Beyond immediate post-merger tasks, long-term tax planning should be established. This includes reviewing and updating the combined entity's overall tax strategy to account for the changes in structure, operations, and ownership. It also involves establishing a clear process for future M&A activity and integrating tax planning into the broader corporate strategy. This could include establishing a dedicated tax committee to provide oversight and guidance.

Moreover, post-merger integration offers a valuable opportunity to streamline tax operations and enhance efficiency. For instance, implementing advanced tax technology solutions can automate several tasks, reduce manual effort, and improve accuracy in tax compliance. Investing in employee training is also a critical element in ensuring that the combined tax team has the skills and knowledge to effectively manage the post-merger tax landscape. This minimizes errors and ensures the seamless integration of processes.

Finally, remember the importance of staying current with tax laws and regulations. Tax laws are constantly evolving, and understanding these changes is essential for ensuring ongoing compliance. This may require engaging with tax professionals and staying informed about updates through professional publications and relevant industry events. Ignoring these updates risks penalties. Continuous learning is crucial in the field of tax.

A well-structured post-merger integration of the tax functions is a cornerstone of a successful merger. The financial gains from a well-executed integration often surpass the initial investment many times over.

5.1 Tax Planning Post-Acquisition

Effective tax planning after an acquisition is crucial for maximizing value and minimizing future tax liabilities. This isn't merely about complying with regulations; it's about strategically positioning the combined entity for long-term financial success. A thorough understanding of the tax implications of the merger or acquisition, as discussed in previous chapters, is paramount to this process.

The initial step involves a comprehensive review of the acquired company's tax records. This includes examining past returns, open tax years, outstanding assessments, and any potential liabilities. Identifying and addressing these issues proactively prevents unexpected surprises down the road, and can often lead to substantial savings by identifying underpayments, overlooked deductions or credits. Such proactive identification can often lead to negotiating favorable terms with tax authorities during subsequent audits and reduce the chances of disputes. This careful review allows for a smooth integration of the two entities' tax structures.

Next, consider optimizing depreciation and amortization schedules. The purchase price allocation (discussed in a previous chapter) directly impacts this. By carefully assigning values to different assets, you can strategically manage depreciation and amortization deductions to reduce your overall tax burden over the coming years. This can potentially create significant tax benefits, provided the allocation is reasonable and justifiable. Consult with tax professionals to ensure compliance with all relevant regulations, and create a plan which optimizes deductions for the newly merged entity's future cash flows.

Integrating the accounting systems of both companies is a vital part of post-acquisition tax planning. Different accounting methods and systems can complicate the reporting process, leading to potential errors and delays in filing. Establishing a standardized system early on streamlines reporting, simplifies compliance, and minimizes the risk of errors. This not only saves time and resources but also significantly reduces the chances of audit flags and penalties. Planning for this transition and coordinating with both companies' internal teams is crucial for efficiency and success.

Furthermore, the post-acquisition period presents an opportunity to reassess and potentially restructure debt obligations. Interest expenses are typically tax-deductible, and a strategic restructuring can lead to increased deductibility, further reducing the overall tax liability. Careful consideration should be given to interest rate and term strategies for both short and long-term liabilities, optimizing for both tax impact and overall financial health. This needs to be undertaken in conjunction with financial modeling and forecasting to evaluate the long term impact. Finally, don't overlook the ongoing compliance requirements. Maintaining meticulous records, filing accurate and timely tax returns, and responding promptly to any tax authority inquiries are essential for avoiding penalties and maintaining a positive relationship with tax agencies. A dedicated compliance team or external advisor is often needed during and after integration to ensure that every aspect of tax law is adhered to. This proactive approach protects the company's reputation and financial stability, ensuring that the benefits gained from tax planning are not jeopardized by administrative oversights. Remember that proactive compliance is not simply about avoiding penalties; it is an essential part of ensuring long-term stability and success. The combined entity must have a proactive post-acquisition tax strategy in place, one that ensures both compliance and optimizes the company's financial prospects.

5.2 Compliance and Reporting

Accurate and timely tax reporting is paramount after a merger or acquisition. Failure to comply with regulations can result in significant penalties, impacting the overall success of the deal. Understanding the intricacies of post-merger reporting requirements is crucial for maintaining regulatory compliance and minimizing financial risks. A well-structured approach is essential.

The immediate post-merger period demands swift action. Consolidating financial records from distinct entities requires a coordinated effort. This involves integrating disparate accounting systems, reconciling accounts, and establishing a unified chart of accounts. Inconsistencies in accounting methods must be addressed proactively. This meticulous process establishes a foundation for accurate reporting. Any delays can complicate the tax reporting process and potentially lead to inaccuracies.

Filing consolidated tax returns is a key aspect of post-merger compliance. This process requires a thorough understanding of the rules governing consolidated tax groups. It involves aggregating the income, deductions, credits, and losses of all entities within the group, filing a single return, and dealing with complex intercompany transactions. Furthermore, each subsidiary must maintain its own records, but these records must be readily accessible to support the consolidated return. The complexity necessitates expert assistance from tax professionals to avoid errors and penalties.

Beyond consolidated returns, accurate reporting encompasses various other tax forms. These might include information returns related to specific transactions or distributions, depending on the specific structure of the deal. Understanding the requirements for each applicable form is critical to preventing compliance issues. Proactive engagement with tax advisors is paramount to navigating this complex regulatory landscape.

State tax compliance adds another layer of complexity. Mergers and acquisitions often involve entities operating in multiple states, demanding adherence to diverse state tax rules and regulations. Each state has its own unique filing requirements, complicating the process further. This demands a thorough understanding of nexus rules and apportionment formulas, as well as meticulous tracking of sales and income within each jurisdiction. Failure to comply with state tax obligations could lead to significant penalties.

The long-term tax implications of a merger or acquisition extend beyond the initial reporting period. Ongoing compliance involves maintaining accurate records, continually monitoring tax law changes, and adapting reporting strategies accordingly. Tax planning is crucial in the post-merger phase. This involves strategically managing deductions, credits, and other tax-related aspects to minimize tax liabilities in the long term. A proactive, long-term tax strategy safeguards future financial well-being.

Proactive engagement with experienced tax professionals is not merely advisable; it's essential. Their expertise in navigating the complexities of post-merger tax compliance is invaluable. They provide guidance on the nuances of regulatory requirements and help ensure accurate and timely filing. Their involvement helps minimize errors and potential disputes with tax authorities, providing peace of mind and focusing on the strategic management of the combined entity.

Transparency and meticulous record-keeping are fundamental. Maintaining complete and accurate records simplifies audits and reduces the likelihood of errors. Establishing robust internal controls and implementing effective documentation practices are vital. This diligent approach ensures that the financial information reported to tax authorities is reliable and defensible. The ability to readily access and provide verifiable data simplifies any interactions with tax authorities.

Ultimately, compliance and accurate reporting are not merely about avoiding penalties. They contribute to the long-term financial health and stability of the newly formed entity. By establishing a solid foundation for post-merger tax management, companies pave the way for sustained growth and success. This meticulous attention to detail reinforces the overall credibility and stability of the business in the eyes of investors, partners, and regulatory bodies. The value of careful planning and accurate reporting cannot be overstated.

6 Valuation and Tax Implications

Accurate valuation is paramount in mergers and acquisitions (M&A), significantly impacting tax liabilities. The Internal Revenue Service (IRS) scrutinizes valuations, so understanding the process is critical for minimizing disputes and ensuring compliance. Fair market value, the price a willing buyer would pay a willing seller in an arm's-length transaction, is the cornerstone of valuation. This isn't a simple calculation; it requires a deep understanding of the target company's financials, market position, and future prospects. Experienced professionals often employ a multi-faceted approach, considering various valuation methodologies, including discounted cash flow analysis, market multiples, and asset-based approaches. The selection depends on the nature of the business and the availability of relevant data. For example, a technology company with substantial intellectual property might require a more nuanced approach compared to a mature manufacturing firm. Discrepancies in valuations can lead to protracted disputes and substantial tax consequences.

Determining the fair market value of intangible assets presents unique challenges. These assets, including trademarks, patents, copyrights, and customer relationships, lack the tangible nature of physical assets. Their value is often derived from their potential to generate future cash flows, making their assessment complex. Methods like relief-from-royalty and income approaches are commonly employed. However, selecting the appropriate methodology and supporting it with credible evidence is crucial. The IRS typically scrutinizes these valuations closely. A poorly supported valuation can result in adjustments to the purchase price allocation, leading to higher tax liabilities. Therefore, meticulous documentation and independent appraisal are essential.

Goodwill, an intangible asset representing the excess of the purchase price over the fair market value of identifiable net assets, plays a significant role in M&A tax implications. While goodwill isn't directly amortized for tax purposes under current US tax law, it's subject to an impairment test. If the value of goodwill declines significantly, a tax deduction may be allowed. However, proving impairment can be difficult and requires substantial evidence. Therefore, understanding goodwill's impact on tax planning, including its potential for future tax benefits or liabilities, is vital. Properly accounting for and justifying the valuation of goodwill is crucial to minimizing potential tax disputes with the IRS. This often involves detailed analysis of market conditions, competitive landscape, and the target company's future financial performance. Ignoring these factors can lead to significant tax penalties.

The interaction between valuation and tax implications is multifaceted and requires careful consideration. For example, the allocation of the purchase price among various assets directly impacts depreciation and amortization deductions. Assigning a higher value to assets with shorter useful lives increases deductions in the earlier years, potentially reducing the overall tax burden. Conversely, assigning a higher value to assets with longer lives might postpone tax benefits. This necessitates a thorough understanding of both tax laws and valuation principles. Optimal allocation requires careful planning and collaboration between valuation specialists and tax advisors, as an incorrect allocation can result in substantial tax deficiencies.

This complex interplay underscores the need for expert advice to ensure compliance with all relevant tax regulations.

Negotiating the purchase price is a critical aspect of M&A transactions and has significant tax ramifications. A higher purchase price may result in a larger tax deduction for depreciation and amortization, but it also increases the buyer's tax basis, potentially affecting future capital gains taxes. Conversely, a lower purchase price may reduce these deductions, and lessen the buyer's ultimate tax burden, but it can also increase the seller's tax liabilities if the gain is less than anticipated. The negotiation process must consider tax implications for both parties, ensuring the deal is not only financially advantageous but also tax-efficient. Understanding these dynamics requires expertise in both taxation and the intricacies of business valuation. This knowledge allows businesses to navigate the complexities of M&A while minimizing tax exposure.

Ultimately, achieving a tax-efficient outcome in an M&A transaction requires a synergistic approach. This involves careful pre-transaction planning, precise valuation, and meticulous purchase price allocation. Engaging qualified professionals in both valuation and tax advisory is not merely a suggestion; it's a necessity. These experts can guide you through the complexities of determining fair market value, optimizing purchase price allocation, and navigating the intricacies of tax laws, ensuring you're well-prepared to handle any audit or IRS examination. Their expertise helps minimize tax liabilities, maximize returns, and ensure a smooth post-merger integration. Ignoring this critical aspect of M&A can lead to costly mistakes and significant tax penalties. Ignoring the crucial synergy between valuation and taxation, in the complex landscape of M&A, can have far-reaching and costly consequences.

6.1 Fair Market Value Determination

Determining fair market value (FMV) is paramount in mergers and acquisitions (M&A), significantly influencing tax liabilities and overall transaction success. A precise FMV assessment ensures fair allocation of the purchase price among assets, directly impacting depreciation and amortization deductions. This directly affects the ultimate tax burden on the acquiring company. Miscalculating FMV can lead to substantial tax penalties and disputes with tax authorities.

Unlike other valuation methods, which may focus on specific aspects of a business, FMV determination considers all relevant factors influencing the value of an asset in an open market transaction between a willing buyer and a willing seller, neither under any compulsion. This "hypothetical" exchange forms the foundation of FMV. It's a conceptual exercise, requiring sophisticated analysis and expertise.

Several approaches exist to determine FMV, each with strengths and limitations depending on the specific asset and circumstances of the transaction. The income approach focuses on the present value of future cash flows. Imagine estimating future profits from a target company's anticipated revenue streams; discounting those projected earnings using an appropriate discount rate results in a valuation. This requires careful consideration of industry benchmarks and macroeconomic factors. The market approach relies on comparable transactions. It involves identifying similar businesses that have recently been sold and using their sale prices as benchmarks, adjusting for any relevant differences. Finding truly comparable businesses can be challenging, demanding detailed research and in-depth industry knowledge. This approach necessitates considering market specific details such as transaction dates, economic conditions, and unique company characteristics.

The asset approach determines value by summing the individual fair market values of an entity's assets. This approach is simpler in principle but can prove complicated in practice, needing exhaustive and meticulous identification and valuation of all assets, both tangible and intangible. For example, determining the FMV of intellectual property requires complex analysis. Often, several approaches are used concurrently, offering a triangulated viewpoint; this method often leads to a more robust and reliable estimate of FMV, although still subject to expert judgment. Using multiple valuation approaches mitigates the risks associated with any single method. Each approach's strengths and weaknesses are assessed and compared to reach the most probable FMV. The final assessment often involves subjective judgment and professional interpretation.

The IRS scrutinizes FMV determinations rigorously, demanding solid documentation and justification for the methodology used. Failure to meet IRS standards can result in costly adjustments and penalties. Proper documentation is critical, not merely for tax compliance, but also to defend the valuation against potential challenges during audits. A thorough valuation report, prepared by a qualified appraiser, outlining the methods used and providing a detailed explanation for each step, forms the strongest defense against an IRS challenge. This report would not only provide justifications for the chosen valuation method, but would also display a complete analysis of the reasoning behind the valuation.

In the context of M&A transactions, determining FMV for intangible assets presents particular challenges. Goodwill, brand recognition, and intellectual property often represent a substantial portion of a company's value. The lack of readily observable market prices for such assets requires more sophisticated valuation methods. These methods usually incorporate complex financial modeling and analysis. In some cases, it might even require engaging specialist valuation firms. In practice, accurate determination of FMV for such intangible assets becomes a process of careful analysis. It is important to carefully research and understand the valuation methods and appropriate regulatory guidance. It's vital to meticulously document the valuation process. A careful approach, using multiple methods, is crucial.

The selection of the valuation method depends significantly on the nature of the assets involved, the availability of market data, and the specific circumstances of the transaction. It is therefore crucial to choose the most appropriate and reliable method, consulting with experienced professionals is often beneficial. It is often recommended to involve valuation experts early in the M&A process to ensure a smooth and compliant transaction. Expert advice aids in navigating the complexities of FMV determination. The correct FMV valuation can save significant tax liabilities and protect against future disputes. Investing in proper valuation expertise at the outset can prove much more cost-effective than addressing disputes and penalties later. The ultimate goal is to arrive at a FMV that is both defensible and minimizes tax consequences for all parties involved in the transaction. Achieving this requires meticulous planning and an understanding of the applicable tax regulations.

6.2 Intangible Asset Valuation

Valuing intangible assets during mergers and acquisitions presents unique challenges. Unlike tangible assets with readily observable market prices, intangible assets like brand recognition, customer relationships, and intellectual property require sophisticated valuation methodologies. A precise valuation is crucial because it directly influences the purchase price allocation, affecting future tax deductions. Incorrect valuation can lead to significant tax liabilities down the line. Therefore, a robust and defensible valuation approach is paramount.

The most common methods for valuing intangible assets include the income approach, the market approach, and the cost approach. The income approach estimates the value based on the future cash flows generated by the asset. This might involve discounted cash flow (DCF) analysis, which forecasts future income streams and discounts them to their present value, considering risk and the time value of money. The selection of a suitable discount rate is critical, as it profoundly impacts the final valuation. A higher discount rate reflects a higher perceived risk and results in a lower present value.

The market approach identifies comparable assets that have been recently sold to determine a market-based valuation. This method is most effective when similar assets have recently changed hands, providing relevant transactional data. However, finding truly comparable assets is often difficult. It requires extensive market research and a careful analysis of the similarities and differences between the subject asset and the comparables. Subjectivity inevitably creeps in. Any differences necessitate adjustments, adding further complexity to the process.

The cost approach determines value by estimating the cost of replacing or reproducing the asset. This method is particularly relevant when the asset is unique or when reliable market data is scarce. The cost approach might involve estimating development costs, research and development expenses, or the cost of establishing similar assets from scratch. It's important to consider factors like obsolescence and technological advancements that can diminish an asset's value.

Regardless of the chosen methodology, thorough documentation is essential. A well-documented valuation report provides transparency and helps defend the valuation in the event of an IRS audit. This report should clearly outline the valuation methodology used, the data employed, and all assumptions made. Supporting documentation, such as market research reports, financial statements, and expert opinions, adds credibility to the valuation. The documentation must be comprehensive and transparent enough to withstand rigorous scrutiny.

Beyond the core methods, other factors influence intangible asset valuation. These include the asset's useful life, which impacts the calculation of amortization deductions. An accurate determination of useful life requires careful consideration of market trends, technological advancements, and the asset's competitive position. Moreover, legal and contractual factors, such as licensing agreements or intellectual property rights, may affect the valuation. The existence of any impediments on the asset's use needs to be carefully considered.

Furthermore, the specific industry context matters significantly. Industry-specific standards and practices often influence the appropriate valuation methods and the data used in the analysis. A deep understanding of the industry in which the asset operates is crucial for an accurate valuation. For example, valuing a pharmaceutical patent requires different methods than valuing a brand name in the consumer goods industry. Expertise in both accounting and the industry is necessary for creating a reliable valuation.

Finally, remember that intangible asset valuation is not an exact science; it often involves some degree of subjectivity and judgment. Expert opinions from qualified professionals are highly advisable, especially in complex transactions involving numerous assets and intricate contractual arrangements. Obtaining multiple independent valuations can help reduce uncertainty and increase the credibility of the valuation. These independent opinions can highlight any potential disagreements and thus help create a more robust analysis. Engaging multiple experts ensures you are prepared for potential disagreements and increases the accuracy of the final valuation.

6.3 Goodwill & Amortization

Goodwill, an intangible asset representing the value of a company beyond its identifiable assets, often arises in mergers and acquisitions. Its valuation is crucial, directly impacting the tax implications for the acquiring company. Determining the fair market value of goodwill requires a rigorous and multifaceted approach, often involving sophisticated valuation techniques and professional expertise. This isn't a simple task, requiring careful consideration of various factors and potential pitfalls.

Unlike tangible assets with clearly defined useful lives, goodwill is typically considered to have an indefinite life. This means it's not subject to amortization under U.S. GAAP (Generally Accepted Accounting Principles). However, for tax purposes, the Internal Revenue Code (IRC) Section 197 mandates amortization of acquired goodwill over a 15-year period. This creates a disparity between financial reporting and tax accounting, necessitating careful planning to mitigate potential discrepancies and optimize tax outcomes.

The amortization deduction allowed under Section 197 provides a significant tax benefit to the acquiring company. This deduction reduces taxable income, leading to lower tax liabilities. However, the amount of this deduction depends directly on the initial valuation of goodwill. An overvaluation leads to higher upfront amortization deductions, resulting in lower current-year tax payments, but potentially higher taxes in subsequent years. Conversely, an undervaluation results in lower initial deductions but could lead to missed tax savings opportunities.

Understanding the interplay between the financial statement presentation of goodwill and its tax amortization is critical. For financial reporting, goodwill remains on the balance sheet until impaired. Tax accounting, however, demands the systematic amortization of goodwill, regardless of impairment. This difference requires careful reconciliation between the two reporting frameworks. Any discrepancies must be meticulously documented and explained in the company's tax filings.

Consider the scenario of a company acquiring another for $100 million. After allocating the purchase price, $20 million might be attributed to goodwill. Under Section 197, this goodwill is amortized over 15 years, resulting in an annual amortization deduction of $1.33 million. This deduction directly reduces the company's taxable income, resulting in a lower tax burden. This seemingly straightforward calculation, however, can become complex when dealing with multiple intangible assets acquired simultaneously.

The process of allocating the purchase price among different assets, including goodwill, is paramount. This purchase price allocation (PPA) is crucial for determining the appropriate tax basis of each asset and directly affects the calculation of amortization deductions. Inaccurate PPA can lead to significant tax errors and potential IRS scrutiny. Therefore, professional advice from experienced tax advisors is highly recommended.

Furthermore, the valuation of goodwill is inherently subjective and relies on various methodologies. Common approaches include discounted cash flow analysis, market multiples, and asset-based valuations. The selection of the appropriate method depends on the specific circumstances of the transaction and the nature of the acquired business. Justifying the chosen valuation method is crucial in the event of an IRS audit.

Tax planning in relation to goodwill and its amortization should be a proactive, not reactive, process. It should begin well before the actual transaction. Experienced tax advisors can help businesses develop strategies to minimize the tax implications related to goodwill, ensuring compliance with all applicable tax regulations. This pre-transaction planning is essential for mitigating future tax risks and optimizing tax benefits.

To summarize, while goodwill, an intangible asset, lacks a physical presence, its implications are very real and far-reaching, particularly in the context of M&A transactions. The understanding and proper handling of its valuation and amortization are crucial for tax compliance and maximizing tax benefits. Careful consideration of the differences between financial reporting and tax treatment is essential, and professional guidance from tax specialists can prove invaluable in navigating the complexities of goodwill and its impact on the overall tax position of the acquiring entity. Ignoring these considerations could lead to significant financial setbacks. Proactive tax planning is the key to optimizing the opportunities presented by goodwill's unique tax treatment, thus safeguarding the financial well-being of the business. Remember, the tax benefits of amortization are only realized through accurate valuation and proper reporting.

7 Dispute Resolution & Litigation

Navigating the complexities of mergers and acquisitions often leads to unforeseen tax challenges. Disputes with the IRS are unfortunately a common occurrence, arising from disagreements over valuations, interpretations of tax law, or even procedural issues during the audit process. Understanding the landscape of dispute resolution and potential litigation is therefore crucial for anyone involved in these high-stakes transactions. Preparation is key, allowing for a more effective and potentially less costly resolution.

The IRS audit process can be daunting. It typically begins with a formal notice, outlining the specific areas under scrutiny. This notice might focus on aspects like purchase price allocation, the valuation of intangible assets, or the proper application of tax codes related to specific merger or acquisition structures. Responding effectively requires meticulous record-keeping and a deep understanding of the transaction's underlying tax implications. You must be able to not only provide supporting documentation but also articulate a clear and defensible rationale for your tax positions.

Proactive measures are far more efficient than reactive responses. A thorough pre-transaction tax planning strategy minimizes the likelihood of future disputes. This proactive approach involves engaging with qualified tax professionals early in the process. Their expertise in structuring transactions to minimize tax risk significantly reduces the chance of an audit. Even after the deal closes, careful compliance and robust record-keeping remain essential to lessen the chance of future complications.

If an audit does occur, the initial response is critical. Gather all relevant documentation promptly, including financial statements, contracts, appraisals, and internal memos. Collaborate closely with your legal and tax advisors to develop a comprehensive strategy. This strategy should address each point of contention raised by the IRS, presenting a clear and well-supported counterargument. Remember, cooperation with the IRS is often beneficial but steadfastly maintaining your positions and protecting your interests are of equal importance.

Escalation to litigation is a last resort, costly and time-consuming. While a negotiated settlement is always preferable, the possibility of litigation requires a robust strategy. This strategy must include a comprehensive understanding of the relevant tax laws, regulations, and case precedents. It's imperative to have a skilled legal team experienced in tax litigation. This team will guide you through the process, representing your interests in court while diligently managing expectations of the potential outcomes. The cost, both financial and emotional, associated with litigation can be considerable, so this possibility needs to be thoroughly considered in your contingency planning.

The process is further complicated by the involvement of multiple parties in typical M&A transactions. Shareholders, boards of directors, and potentially even the acquiring or target company's employees all may have vested interests in the outcome of a tax dispute. These disparate interests can lead to internal conflicts, further complicating the resolution process. This complexity highlights the value of proactive legal and tax counsel to align the interests of all involved parties and to foster a consistent response strategy.

Ultimately, the best approach to dispute resolution and potential litigation is prevention. A well-defined tax strategy, implemented with the guidance of experienced professionals, reduces the risk of audits and subsequent disputes significantly. This means more than just compliance with the letter of the law—it also involves a deep understanding of the spirit of the law and proactively addressing potential areas of contention. It's a matter of carefully navigating the intricate web of tax regulations that govern mergers and acquisitions, ensuring not just legal compliance, but also long-term tax efficiency.
The financial stakes in mergers and acquisitions are often substantial. A successful outcome hinges not only on achieving the strategic objectives of the transaction but also on effectively managing the related tax implications. Addressing potential tax disputes proactively through careful planning and a strategic approach can safeguard the overall success of the transaction, protecting both the financial and reputational interests of all involved parties. By understanding the process from start to finish, preparing for potential challenges, and choosing the right professional guidance, you substantially increase the likelihood of favorable resolutions when dealing with tax controversies. This proactive approach will minimize disruption to your business and safeguard your financial well-being in the event of a dispute with the IRS. Remember, a well-prepared defense is often the best offense.

7.1 IRS Audits & Examinations

Navigating an IRS audit following a merger or acquisition can be daunting, but proactive preparation significantly improves your chances of a positive outcome. The IRS scrutinizes these transactions closely, seeking to ensure accurate reporting of all assets and liabilities, and the proper application of tax laws. Understanding the process and assembling the necessary documentation beforehand is crucial. This includes meticulously documenting all aspects of the transaction, from initial negotiations to the final closing.

Your response to an audit summons should be prompt and comprehensive. Delaying or ignoring the request could escalate the situation and lead to more severe penalties. Gather all relevant documentation, including the purchase agreement, financial statements, tax returns, and any appraisals or valuations performed during the transaction. Organize these documents logically, making them easily accessible for the IRS examiners.

Consider engaging experienced tax professionals. They can provide invaluable guidance throughout the audit process, ensuring you understand your rights and obligations. Their expertise in tax law, specifically related to M&A transactions, is indispensable in navigating complex regulations and interpreting IRS requests. A qualified professional can also represent your interests during any discussions with the IRS, providing a critical buffer between you and the examining agent.

Remember, the IRS audit is not necessarily adversarial. Cooperation and a transparent approach often lead to more favorable outcomes. Be honest and forthcoming with the examiners, answering their questions fully and accurately. If you encounter questions you cannot immediately answer, it's acceptable to request time to collect the necessary information, keeping careful records of this exchange.

While proactive preparation is key, even the most meticulous documentation may not prevent an IRS challenge. The valuation of assets and liabilities, particularly intangible assets like goodwill, is often a point of contention. Be prepared to justify your valuations with robust evidence, relying on reliable methods and qualified appraisals. Independent appraisals can be extremely useful in presenting a clear and supportable position.

During the examination, maintain detailed records of all communications and requests. Note the date, time, and specifics of any discussions with IRS examiners, including the identities of those involved. This meticulous record-keeping will protect your interests should the audit escalate into a legal dispute. A thorough record also assists your legal team in representing your position accurately and effectively.

Understanding the potential issues is paramount. Common IRS audit focuses include the proper allocation of the purchase price, the accurate determination of the tax basis of assets, and the correct application of relevant tax codes. Knowing these potential areas of scrutiny allows you to strengthen your defense by ensuring a comprehensive documentation strategy, addressing these points meticulously during the process.

The ultimate goal in dealing with an IRS audit is resolution. While some disputes may lead to litigation, many are resolved through negotiation and compromise. Be willing to explore all options for settlement, but only accept agreements that reflect a fair and accurate assessment of your tax liability. Consider seeking legal counsel to understand any options available, as a legal professional can provide indispensable assistance in negotiating or fighting tax-related disputes.

Remember that even with meticulous preparation and professional representation, audits can be stressful. Maintaining clear communication with your team and staying organized throughout the process is crucial to mitigating stress and ensuring the best possible outcome. By proactively addressing potential issues and focusing on transparency, you can navigate this challenging situation effectively and minimize potential financial and legal ramifications. A robust defense, supported by clear documentation and competent professional advice, greatly increases your chances of a favorable resolution. Proactive steps taken before, during, and after the acquisition process significantly reduce the likelihood of future difficulties. The cost of preventing an audit is far less than resolving a conflict. Prioritize meticulous record-keeping and sound financial planning.

7.2 Tax Controversy

Navigating a tax controversy after a merger or acquisition can be daunting, especially for those new to the complexities of business transactions. It's a landscape filled with IRS scrutiny, intricate regulations, and potentially significant financial ramifications. Understanding the process, from initial audit to potential litigation, is key to minimizing damage and achieving a favorable outcome. Preparation is paramount; proactively organizing financial records, ensuring meticulous documentation of all transactions, and maintaining open communication with your tax advisor can significantly reduce the likelihood of disputes.

A thorough understanding of the specific tax laws governing your particular transaction is essential. This requires more than just a cursory review; it involves a deep dive into relevant codes, regulations, and precedents. Different jurisdictions have varying rules; international transactions, for example, introduce a whole new layer of complexity involving treaties and foreign tax credits. Seeking professional advice from experienced tax attorneys specializing in M&A is not a luxury but a necessity. They can provide guidance on navigating intricate tax codes and represent your interests effectively in any conflict.

The IRS audit process can be intimidating. It begins with a notification, often followed by a request for extensive documentation. Responding promptly and comprehensively is critical. Failing to comply can escalate the situation, resulting in penalties and potentially more serious repercussions. Your tax advisor will guide you through this process, helping you gather and present the necessary information in a clear and organized manner. This ensures transparency and cooperation, often improving the chances of a positive resolution without lengthy legal battles.

If an audit leads to a disagreement, the process might move into the appeals process within the IRS itself. This stage offers an opportunity for negotiation and compromise before escalating to the courts. Know your rights, understand the IRS's procedures, and prepare a strong case with your legal team. Effective communication, clear presentation of evidence, and a willingness to engage in good-faith negotiation can frequently resolve disputes at this level. However, preparation for more involved legal battles is necessary.

If the appeals process fails to yield a resolution, you might face tax litigation. This is a serious step, often requiring extensive resources and legal expertise. Gathering and presenting evidence, understanding the court's procedures, and preparing for rigorous questioning is all part of the process. Your legal team will play a crucial role in building your defense and presenting your case persuasively before the judge. Legal strategies will depend on the specifics of your case, including potential avenues for settlement.

Remember, preventative measures are far more effective than reactive ones. Thorough due diligence during the pre-merger or acquisition phase helps identify potential tax risks early on. Employing experienced tax professionals from the outset minimizes the chance of future disputes. By structuring the transaction strategically and documenting everything meticulously, you can significantly reduce the risk of running into complex tax issues. A proactive approach, supported by sound legal and financial counsel, is your best defense against a tax controversy. Remember, the goal isn't just to win the dispute; it's to preserve the financial health of your organization. Effective tax planning and proactive management can ultimately save you time, money, and considerable stress. The peace of mind achieved by anticipating and mitigating potential problems is invaluable in the long run. Navigating the complexities of M&A requires preparation, expertise, and a proactive mindset.

www.ingramcontent.com/pod-product-compliance
Lightning Source LLC
LaVergne TN
LVHW022027200926
848481LV00007B/2577

* 9 7 9 8 3 4 9 3 0 5 2 0 7 *